Flower Days

An Origami-Inspired
Creativity Journal

KUMIKO SUDO

Breckling Press

This book was set in Cochin by Bartko Design, Inc.
Editorial direction by Anne Knudsen
Art direction, cover and interior design by Kim Bartko
Interior illustrations by Kandy Petersen
Cover illustration by Kumiko Sudo

Published by Breckling Press
283 Michigan St.
Elmhurst, IL 60126 USA

Printed and bound in China
International Standard Book Number: 0-9721-2187-0

I am often asked where ideas for new designs come from. My answer is that inspiration requires a deep sensitivity toward the world around us. I try to open my eyes to wildflowers that cling to pathways, seedlings ready to fall from withered plants, or tiny clusters of moss on the surface of a tree trunk. If I look and listen, not just with my eyes and ears but with my heart, an image of a new blossom takes shape in my mind—an image that will bloom again for me in fabric.

Introduction

FOR AS LONG AS I REMEMBER, the written word, with its power to capture stories and memories, has been an important part of my life. As very young children, my sister and I would create our own storybooks, filling page after page with pictures and with our naïve interpretations of the world around us. When I was eight years old, I moved from the bustling city of Tokyo to live with my aunt in the quiet mountains of Kamakura. It was there that I began to keep notebooks of my thoughts to share with my mother when she visited. As well as being a place to record my innocent observations of daily life, my notebooks became a doorway into a fantasy world. I made up little fables about the flowers in our woodland home and about the creatures that lived among them. I do the same today, and the joy I feel in the stories becomes part of my work and adds a special texture to the quilts and flowers I make from fabric.

Recording my thoughts has become an experience that has enriched my life by helping me see and understand the world around me. I am often asked how I develop ideas for new designs. Although it is so natural to me that I do not consider it a technique, I find that my routine of keeping notes gives me a constant source of inspiration. Spontaneity is very important. I never pressure myself to produce an idea—this doesn't work because the idea must come naturally. I usually keep small notepads in handy places, and every time I come up with an idea—no matter how minimal it may seem—I make a sketch and include the date. I also jot down my thoughts and impressions. Later, I go through those thumbnail sketches and transform them into larger forms. Sometimes, I combine several sketches in various ways and these combinations result in new, unexpected designs.

I encourage you to use this notebook to help you look at the world through new eyes. Write down your impressions, your experiences, and your deepest thoughts. Keep notes of colors you enjoy, shapes that entrance you, or images you would like to recreate. Stories, too, are a powerful way to preserve memories or look at life from a fresh perspective. In the blank pages at the back of the journal, draw sketches—no matter how rough—and let them evolve over time into new designs. Like me, you will find that when you are ready to develop an idea, your notes will be an amiable companion and a rich source of inspiration.

Kumiko Sudo

Origami Flowers

THE TEN DESIGNS INCLUDED in *Flower Days* were first published in my books *Folded Flowers* and *Flower Origami*. My reason for including them in this journal is simple. Sometimes, in order to write our thoughts or impressions of the world, it is necessary to achieve a tranquil state of mind. Words written in haste or under the pressure of being "creative," seldom reflect our innermost selves. I find that working with fabric is very calming. To help me collect my thoughts for my journal or for a new story, I sometimes hold a piece of fabric and fold it into new shapes. The concerns of the day fly from my mind and I am soon ready for quiet moments of meditation.

You may experiment with the origami designs in fabric or—if you wish—in paper. Some of the designs—Sun Rose, Iris, and Mallow Rose, for instance, work out beautifully when made from double-sided origami paper. Others, like Phlox, Pompon Dahlia, or Delphinium, are better suited to fabric, which is supple and easier to manipulate than a crisp sheet of paper. To begin, simply sew together two of the required starter shapes (circles, squares, pentagons, hexagons, or octagons) by taking a running stitch around the perimeter. Leave a couple of inches open, then turn right side out and blind stitch the opening closed. Press the resulting two-sided shape, and you are ready to gently fold your fabric into a flower.

Date _____

SUN ROSE

Sew two circles together

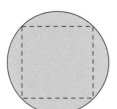

Mark if needed

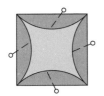

Fold, press, pin

Date _____

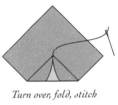

Turn over, fold, stitch

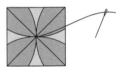

Complete

Date_____

Date

Date _____

Date _____

Date _____

As I work with fabric, I picture the delicate shapes and colors of the
flowers that awaken each month in my garden. In layer after layer,
my fingers fold the fabric and a new blossom comes to life in my hand.

Date_____

Date_____

Date

Date _____

Date _____

PHLOX

Sew two pentagons together

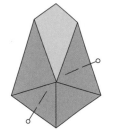

Fold

Fold, press, stitch

Date _____

Roll petal back

Stitch

Date_____

Date

Date

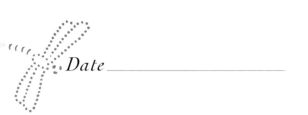

Date _____

Date _____

....
....
....
....
....
....
....
....

If you carefully observe the flowers in your own garden, you will see that they change from day to day. Bud upon bud, a flower opens up to the sun. As the outer petals die, you will see new blossoms at its core. The delicate shades of color, the subtle variations in shape and form, and the changing intensity of fragrance from one day to the next make each moment that you view a flower unique.

Date _____

Date _____

Date _____

Date _____

Date _____

GLADIOLUS

Sew two squares together

Mark or crease if needed

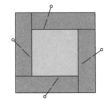

Fold, press, pin

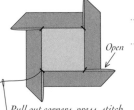

Open

Pull out corners, press, stitch

Date _____

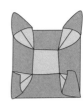

Make peak

Flatten peak into corner square, press, pin

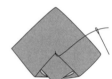

Turn over, fold, stitch

Fold, stitch

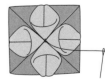

Complete

Date _____

Date _____

Date _____

*Date*_____

Date _____

_____
_____
_____
_____
_____
_____
_____
_____
_____
_____

Observing the loveliness of nature helps me understand the interplay of colors and the balance of design compositions. I am convinced that every one of my design ideas has its inspiration in the flowers, the trees, and the little creatures that inhabit my garden.

Date _____

Date _____

Date_____

Date_____

Date _____

*Date*_____

DELPHINIUM

Sew two octagons together

Mark or crease, fold, press,
pin all sides

Diagonal fold, press, pin

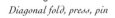

Date _____

Repeat all diagonals

Turn over, fold, stitch

Complete

Date _____

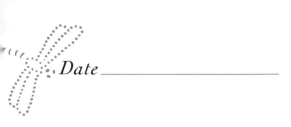

Date _____

Date _____

Date_____

Date _____

When I work with fabric, I think not only of the flowers I wish to create, but of the richness of the natural world. Sunlight, shadows, the fluttering of a bird's wings, the feeling of early morning mist in the air, and the call of the cricket to the autumn moon — all influence the impressions I have of the flowers in my garden.

Date

Date _____

Date _____

Date

Date _____

MALALUECA

Sew two circles together

Mark or crease, fold, press, pin

Turn over, fold to center

Date _____

Back view

Gather at top, stitch to hold

Open out

Date_____

Date _____

Date_____

Date _____

Date _____

....
....
....
....
....
....
....
....

I am often asked how I am able to pick out combinations of colors and fabrics that almost instantly meld into balanced designs. The only answer I am able to offer is that my color sense is intuitive. As unreasonable as this at first sounds, I try to explain that intuition is cultivated over a long period of time, fueled by a variety of sensations and experiences. It blossoms in my mind, year after year, and is expressed through the work I do with my hands.

Date _____

Date _____

Date _____

Date _____

Date _____

Date _____

STAR ALLIUM

Sew two circles together

Mark or crease

Fold, press, pin

*Date*_____

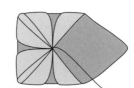

Turn over, fold, stitch

Complete stitching

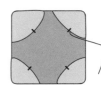

Stitch at back

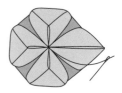

At front, fold in tips

Complete

Date _____

Date_____

Date _____

Date _____

Date _____

....

....

....

....

....

....

....

In choosing colors, I usually follow my intuition. At other times, I am influenced by the mood of the day or the effects of the season. When I feel a gentle spring breeze, for instance, it may suggest pastel colors. If my mood is calm and tranquil, I may choose dramatic color combinations. Beautiful color schemes do not always suggest themselves immediately. I find it takes time and constant rearranging until I am completely satisfied with the way colors and shapes work together.

Date _____

Date

Date_____

Date _____

Date _____

*Date*_____

POMPON DAHLIA

Sew two octagons together

Fold, stitch

Fold, stitch

Date _____

Fold, stitch

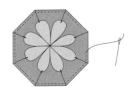

*Open out, stitch at tips
and sides*

Gather, stitch to hold

Date _____

Date _____

Date _____

Date _____

Date _____

Color is a gift of nature and it is waiting for you in your own garden.
Look carefully at the colors in a single flower. Each blossom offers an
incredible range of hues, from the sun-kissed outer petals to the
unfolding bud at the center. Dewdrops, sunlight, and evening shade
subtly alter the tones, bringing endless variety to the impression a
flower makes. You need look no further for a color palette.

Date _____

Date _____

Date _____

Date_____

Date _____

*Date*_____

IRIS

Sew two circles together

Mark or crease, fold, press

Fold, press, pin

Date _____

Fold, press, pin

Fold, press, pin

Fold, stitch

Complete

Date _____

Date _____

Date _____

Date_____

Date _____

_____
_____
_____
_____
_____
_____
_____
_____
_____

Many of my designs begin as sketches. I might come across a beautiful fabric that makes an impression on me. I make a rough sketch of the design. Then I work on refining it, scribbling on endless sheets of paper. In time, I am able to transform it into a full-size design, ready to rework again into fabric.

Date _____

Date _____

Date _____

Date _____

Date _____

*Date*_____

CAMPANULA

Sew two hexagons together

Fold, sew dart

Press dart, stitch

Date _____

Fold, pin

Fold, pin

Gather, stitch to hold

Date _____

Date

Date_____

Date _____

....

....

....

....

....

....

....

....

....

As I work on quilts, I often create stories to go with them. For instance, the very first quilt I made after moving from Japan to the US portrayed a turbulent seascape, the waves pulling in opposite directions. The quilt told the story of the inner struggle I was experiencing — while I was excited about beginning a new life, I longed for my past life in Japan.

Date _____

Date_____

*Date*_____

Date _____

Date _____

MALLOW ROSE

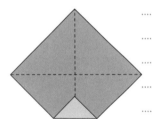

Sew two squares together

Mark or crease if needed, fold

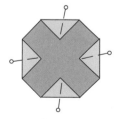

Fold, press, pin

Fold, press, pin

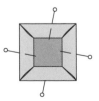

Repeat all sides

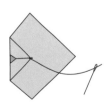

Turn over, fold, press, stitch

Repeat all corners

*Fold inwards to diagonal,
stitch, press*

*Repeat all diagonals. Make
tucks from back and stitch
for rounded shape*

Complete

Date _____

Date_____

Date

Date _____

Date _____

....
....
....
....
....
....
....
....
....

*As I work on new designs, my memories sit beside me. I remember
moments in my life when I felt most at peace with the world around
me and when I found special delight in nature's gifts. I try to
transfer the feelings of warmth my memories bring into the flowers
I create from fabric.*

Date _____

Date _____

Date _____

I learn from nature as it unfolds before me. Flowers bloom but briefly. The images I create in fabric are my attempt to prolong that short, sweet life.

Date of sketch _____

Date of sketch _____

Date of sketch _____

Date of sketch _____

Date of sketch _____

Date of sketch _____

Date of sketch _____

Date of sketch _____

Date of sketch  _____

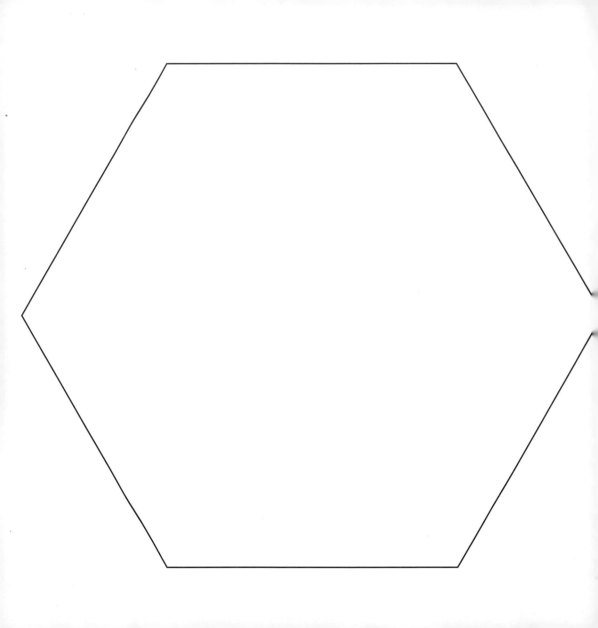

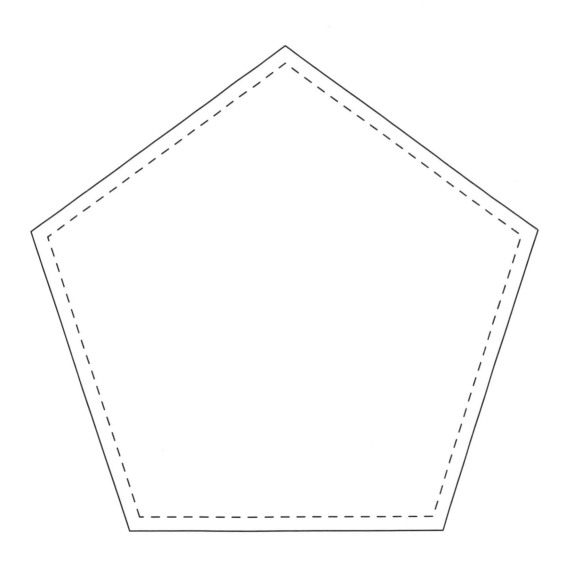

About the Author

KUMIKO SUDO is an internationally acclaimed quilt and fiber artist. Before moving to the United States in 1985, she was known by quilters and fiber artists throughout Japan for her books and was a popular presenter on Japanese national television. Today, Ms. Sudo's work is in several prestigious public and private collections throughout the United States, including the Museum of American Folk Art in New York City. Her books, including bestsellers *Flower Origami, Folded Flowers, Omiyage, Fabled Flowers,* and *East Quilts West,* have inspired quilters and artists around the world. Ms. Sudo lives in Eugene, Oregon.

Also by Kumiko Sudo

Flower Origami: Fabric Flowers from Simple Shapes
Flower Origami Templates: Multi-size Templates for Squares, Circles,
*   Pentagons, and Octagons*
Folded Flowers: Fabric Origami with a Twist of Silk Ribbon

For more information, call 800 951 7836 or visit www.brecklingpress.com.